A busy day in the 1880s brings wagons of every description to Military Plaza, San Antonio's central transportation point which became the site of City Hall.

San Antonio

OUTPOST of EMPIRES

Lewis F. Fisher

Maverick Publishing Company

MAVERICK PUBLISHING COMPANY
P.O. Box 6355, San Antonio, Texas 78209

ALSO BY LEWIS F. FISHER

Crown Jewel of Texas: The Story of San Antonio's River

Saving San Antonio: The Precarious Preservation of a Heritage

Publisher's Cataloging-in-Publication Data

Fisher, Lewis F.
   San Antonio : outpost of empires / Lewis F. Fisher
-- 1st ed.
p. cm.
Includes index.
LCCN: 97-74581
ISBN 0-9651507-3-9
ISBN (pbk.) 0-9651507-4-7

1. San Antonio (Tex.)--History.   I. Title.

F394.S2F57 1997   976.4'351
                         QBI97-41136

06 05 04 03 02 01 00 99 98   10 9 8 7 6 5 4 3 2

Printed in the United States of America
on acid-free paper

Acknowledgments
   Much appreciation goes to those who helped track down illustrations for this book, in particular Tom Shelton at the University of Texas Institute of Texan Cultures at San Antonio; Rebecca Hufstuttler at the Witte Museum; Martha Utterback at the Daughters of the Republic of Texas Library at the Alamo; Nelle Lee Weincek at the San Antonio Conservation Society Library; Mary Alice Harper and Leslie Wearb at the University of Texas at Austin's Harry Ransom Humanities Research Center; Linda Peterson at the University of Texas at Austin's Center for American History; and John Manguso and Jackie Davis at the Fort Sam Houston Military Museum. Thanks for backup go, as always, to my wife Mary and our sons William and Maverick.

Contents

The French tricolor flies over the Alamo as French Marshal Ferdinand Foch, the supreme Allied commander who turned the tide of World War I, is greeted during a drizzle in 1921 at the place where San Antonians traditionally welcome visiting heroes. As this photograph by E. O. Goldbeck shows, this time the stands were built inside remaining walls of the convento of the Spanish Mission San Antonio de Valero, founded with the City of San Antonio in 1718.

Introduction

Born a pawn in the quarrelings of Spain and France for dominion, San Antonio had a troubled youth.

In the space of less than 50 years its parent government changed five times. From 1820 to 1865 San Antonio owed allegiance first to Spain, then to Mexico, then to the Republic of Texas, then to the United States, then to the Confederacy and then, finally, to the United States again.

Geographically isolated from the mainstream of whatever nation or empire had guardianship, and the site of no fewer than six bloody battles for its custody, San Antonio's mixed parentage gives those who would describe the place a hard time.

One early visitor thought San Antonio "a wretched collection of huts" about the time that another, witnessing the beauty of the five Spanish missions, rhapsodized that he could be in Italy.

Zebulon Pike discovered a fiesta spirit, with the Spanish governor dancing in the streets with his subjects, while Sidney Lanier later detected a "bizarre" atmosphere from "the rushing conflux of Americans, Mexicans, Germans, Frenchmen, Swedes, Norwegians, Italians and Negroes."

San Antonio's mixed parentage gives those who would describe the place a hard time.

In 1928 the 30-story Smith-Young Tower—soon to be joined by three others higher than 20 stories—prepares to become San Antonio's tallest building for the next 60 years.

San Antonio is too far west to be southern and too far east to be southwestern, too far from the Rio Grande to be a border city yet close enough to capture a sense of Mexico.

Mid-nineteenth-century visitor Frederick Law Olmsted, soon to design New York City's Central Park, perhaps said it best when he described San Antonio's remote "jumble of races, costumes, languages and buildings" as so picturesque that in America only New Orleans could compare with San Antonio in "odd and antiquated foreignness."

San Antonio's roots were planted too far north for it to grow into an archetypical Spanish colonial town as planned, and it became too civilized by European immigrants to be dismissed as a brawling frontier settlement.

San Antonio is too far west to be characteristically southern and too far east to be completely southwestern, too far from the Rio Grande to be a border city yet close enough to capture a sense of Mexico, too far from major transportation routes to be a world-class commercial center, but big enough to be the nation's ninth-largest city.

A million people may live in San Antonio, but their makeup, too, does not fit common patterns—55 percent Hispanic, 37 percent Anglo, 7 percent black, 1 percent other. The charm of its multicultural heritage makes San Antonio one of the most visited cities in America.

Though the city evolved under a succession of real and would-be empires, none erased the mark of the others. Indeed, among the nation's major cities with Spanish roots San Antonio uniquely retains its Spanish heritage—not just in its name or in the survival of the Spanish tongue, but in the ongoing patterns of daily life.

For San Antonio still functions around a core of streets and plazas in the manner intended by the Spaniards who arranged its civilian, military and religious functions nearly three centuries ago.

Governing councils—both city and county—still meet, as at the beginning, in buildings on the main civilian plaza, even now commanded by the towers of the historic parish church-turned-cathedral of San Fernando. Soldiers may no longer be stationed on the military plaza nearby, but the original residence of their commander remains.

Across downtown, high above the banks of a river that now gives economic rather than bodily nourishment to the city, still stands the church of the Mission San Antonio de Valero, in latter days revered as the Alamo.

A look into San Antonio's past becomes to a very real extent a look at the present, and the future, of this venerable outpost of empires.

Christianizing the natives and turning them into farmers to settle the frontier was the goal of San Antonio's five Spanish missions, including San José, above, founded in 1719.

1. San Antonio de Béxar

Pools of clear water rimmed by thick stands of oaks, pecans and elms marked the lush headwaters of the San Antonio River in 1691 when a group of Spaniards crossing the broad South Texas plain happened by.

It was June 13. That was all Father Damian Massanet needed to decide where the expedition was. "I named this place San Antonio de Padua," he wrote, "because it was his day."

The place named for Saint Anthony was already known as Yanaguana by bands of nomadic Indians, who for thousands of years had been camping at the headwaters and along the tree-lined banks, which formed a ribbon of green as the stream wound lazily toward the Gulf of Mexico 100 miles to the southeast.

Now the newly named San Antonio de Padua was caught up in the clash of distant empires. Father Massanet was traveling with the party of the Spanish governor, Don Domingo de Terán, heading to the East Texas border with the French stronghold of Louisiana.

Six years earlier, the ill-fated LaSalle expedition had landed on the Texas coast, ostensibly off course while looking for the mouth of the Mississippi River. The incident agitated Spanish leaders, who were well aware of the difficulty of defending the empty reaches north of their flourishing silver-mining cities in what is now central Mexico.

Without an adequate number of Spanish colonists to secure the distant frontier, a three-pronged imperial policy was cobbled together in Madrid. It was unique in the New World by including Native Americans rather than seeking to displace them from the land.

Defenders of the Spanish crown would become, quite simply, the Native Americans themselves. They would be

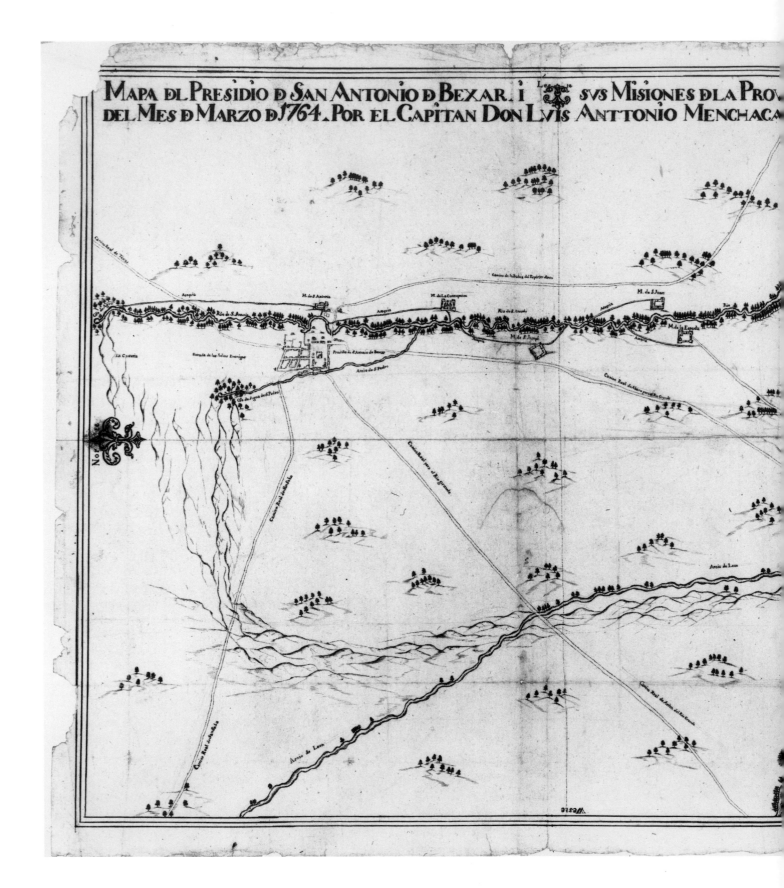

San Antonio, its river and the missions looking east, as drawn by a Spanish army officer in 1764.

gathered in mission communities and converted to Christianity, and would learn the principles of farming before being settled in new communities loyal to Spain throughout the frontier.

Second, to protect the missions and keep an eye on things, soldiers would be garrisoned in nearby presidios.

Third, once Indian farmers had established towns, Spanish colonists—not having to endure the hardships of starting from scratch—would be attracted to the new civilian communities. These towns would be laid out according to the Laws of the Indies, promulgated in 1573 by Spain's Philip II and based upon newly rediscovered Roman urban planning principles.

An eager arm of the imperial policy was the Roman Catholic Church, which could establish and administer the missions from two Franciscan colleges north of Mexico City, at Querétero and Zacatecas.

An obvious place for missions to provide Spain's first line of defense against France was East Texas, which is where the Terán expedition was heading when it came upon the San Antonio River. Two priests, Antonio Olivares and Isidoro Espinosa, later visited the site of San Antonio and thought a strategic waystation should be built where the headwaters of the San Antonio River and its nearby tributary, San Pedro Creek, could support a strong community.

So it was that on May 1, 1718, Father Olivares arrived near the site designated San Antonio de Padua to establish a mission he named San Antonio de Valero, astutely substituting for Padua the name of the viceroy of New Spain, the Marques de Valero. Four days later came the new governor, Martín de Alarcón, to set up a presidio he named San Antonio de Béjar in honor of the viceroy's late brother, the Duque de Béjar (Béxar), a Spanish hero who had died fighting the Turks in Hungary.

Two years later a second mission—San José y San Miguel de Aguayo—was founded farther down the river by one of New Spain's great Franciscan missionaries, Father Antonio Margil de Jesús, who arrived in San Antonio on foot from Zacatecas a half century before another priest, Father Junípero Serra, left Querétero on a similar mission to Upper California.

Grand though the imperial policy may have been, it was not easy to carry out. The distant East Texas missions, supplied only with great difficulty, were hard to defend from Indian attacks. San Antonio, however, had a willing source of converts among tribes like the peaceful

When three missions were moved from East Texas, San Antonio got the largest concentration of Spansh missions in the present-day United States. Clockwise from left top of the facing page are early views of mission churches of San Antonio de Valero, Concepción, San José and Espada. San Juan is shown above.

Founder of San José, the most successful Spanish mission in Texas, was Father Antonio Margil, who came on foot from the Franciscan college at Zacatecas.

Coahuiltecans, who found the missions a refuge from their warlike neighbors, the Comanches and Apaches.

Thus San Antonio became the fallback location for three East Texas missions—Nuestra Señora de la Purisima Concepción de Acuña, San Francisco de la Espada and San Juan Capistrano, all relocated in 1731 along the San Antonio River south of the town.

That same year, on March 7, San Antonio welcomed its only contingent of Spanish immigrants to fulfill the third element of Spanish colonial policy by enlarging the civilian community. This was a group of 55 colonists from the Canary Islands, who were compensated for not having arrived in the settled community they expected by being awarded the noble rank of hidalgo.

Despite the best plans, large numbers of Indians would never move from the missions to become Christianized farmers and townspeople. San Antonio's five missions did flourish, their peak years between 1730 and 1775. Several thousand Indians, baptized, learned to raise livestock and crops and dug the ditches of an intricate acequia water system based on principles perfected in Moorish Spain.

But lacking immunity to European diseases, the Indian ranks were regularly decimated by epidemics. By the end of the eighteenth century San Antonio's mission system had collapsed, although some Indian families continued to stay near the missions, where their descendants still live.

Nor were the military and civilian elements of San Antonio all they were intended to be. The handful of

THREE TOP: COURTESY OF THE WITTE MUSEUM, SAN ANTONIO, TEXAS; LOWER LEFT, SAN ANTONIO CONSERVATION SOCIETY; LOWER RIGHT, THE SAN ANTONIO LIGHT COLLECTION, THE INSTITUTE OF TEXAN CULTURES; ABOVE, ART COLLECTION, HARRY RANSOM HUMANITIES RESEARCH CENTER, THE UNIVERSITY OF TEXAS AT AUSTIN

Independent of San Antonio's mission system was the civilian Villa of San Fernando de Béxar, its focal point the parish church, left, finished in 1749. The villa's homes included La Quinta (1761), right, as painted by Rolla Taylor, on the banks of the San Antonio River. When water was not close at hand an acequia system was built. Mission Espada's included a landmark aqueduct, lower left.

Naming of the Villa of San Fernando honored the royal heir who became Spain's King Ferdinand VI.

Spanish soldiers at the presidio complained of low pay, poor housing, dangerous duty and outrageous prices charged by civilian merchants.

The Canary Islanders, in turn, complained that the soldiers were arrogant and corrupt. The immigrants sparred over grazing and water rights with the mission priests, who kept to themselves and jealously guarded the labors of their Indian converts.

But a civilian government was set up as directed, one of the middle rank—a villa—between the smaller pueblo and the larger ciudad, the latter designation rarely made within the borders of the present-day United States. It was named the Villa of San Fernando de Béxar to honor the royal heir who later became Ferdinand VI.

As prescribed by the Laws of the Indies, the Villa of San Fernando was laid out around a central plaza—La Plaza de las Islas, or Main Plaza—with streets diverging from the plaza made narrow to minimize direct exposure to the burning summer sun.

At the western side of the plaza the parish church was built. Behind the church was a second plaza—La Plaza de Armas, or Military Plaza, headquarters of the presidio.

To the east of the new villa, across the Great Bend of the San Antonio River, was the Mission San Antonio de Valero, later known as the Alamo. It had been relocated from its original site near the springs of San Pedro Creek.

Cut off from the nearest link with civilization—New Orleans—by rivalry with the French, and from the nearest towns in Mexico by several hundred miles of arid, empty

Of San Antonio's three major Spanish-era residences, only the Spanish Governor's Palace (1749), shown above left after its restoration in 1931, has survived. Others were the Veramendi House (ca. 1810), left below, and the de la Garza House (1734), above.

In 1772 the Spanish capital of Texas was moved to San Antonio.

brushlands, the outpost of San Antonio did not make an impressive sight for those able to get there.

Forty years after the Canary Islanders arrived, one visiting priest found "fifty-nine houses of stone and mud and seventy-nine of wood, but all poorly built, without any preconceived plan, so that the whole resembles more a poor village than a villa. . . . The streets are tortuous and filled with mud when it rains."

Marking the skyline was the tower of the church of San Fernando, finished in 1749, its rough local design no match for the delicate Spanish Baroque stonework of the mission churches designed by church architects to the south.

There were two large one-story residences of plastered rock—the de la Garza House where Spanish coins were minted and, facing Military Plaza, the home of the presidio captain, romanticized in its latter-day restoration as the Spanish Governor's Palace.

San Antonio's most impressive Spanish-era home, the Veramendi House, with its large inner courtyard, would be built after the turn of the nineteenth century.

San Antonio's economy was supported simply by the military payroll and by the sale to the south of what livestock could escape Indian raids and get to Spanish towns, where, in any event, homegrown livestock usually brought lower prices than that driven from the north.

Nevertheless, San Antonio continued to grow. Its population had reached 2,000 by the time Louisiana was transferred from France to Spain after the French and Indian War.

The shift cost East Texas its strategic importance. In 1772 the provincial capital was moved from East Texas to San Antonio. That San Antonio was the most important

settlement in Texas was "an almost empty honor," noted one urban historian, "for there existed few competitors."

By the dawn of the nineteenth century, revolutions in British America and France had emboldened revolutionaries in Spanish America.

In 1810, a Spanish Republican refugee who had fled across the border raised an army of American adventurers and some Mexican refugees. The men crossed over to liberate Texas, reaching San Antonio de Béxar, which was sympathetic to the Republicans, in the spring of 1813.

Twice Republicans defeated Royalists in battles near San Antonio, only to be crushed by an army sent up from central Mexico. Hundreds of local Republicans and suspected sympathizers were summarily executed.

Afterward, the Royalist commander, General Joaquín de Arredondo, was based permanently in San Antonio. He remained suspicious of all Americans. But Arredondo also had to cope with warlike Indians to the north.

In December of 1820 the commander was visited in San Antonio by an American, Moses Austin, who asked to bring 300 Anglo-American families to central Texas. There, Austin argued, they would make a fine buffer against the Comanches. Spain, after all, was not coming up with any colonists on its own.

Arredondo finally agreed. Austin got his permission just as the sun was beginning to go down on the Spanish empire in the New World.

Twice Spanish Republicans defeated Spanish Royalists in battles near San Antonio, only to be crushed by an army sent from the south.

In the closing days of Spanish rule over Mexico, Moses Austin came to San Antonio and won permission to bring colonists from the United States into Texas. Austin died less than six months later, leaving son Stephen to establish the colony, and is memorialized in this statue facing the Spanish Governor's Palace.

Mexican President Antonio López de Santa Anna, right, marched north as commander of an army to avenge the surrender of his brother-in-law, General Martín Perfecto de Cós, at a house in San Antonio's La Villita, shown above before its restoration.

2. The Siege of Béxar

Born of rivalry between two European powers, the outpost of San Antonio de Béxar again found itself a crossroads in the struggles for empire when Mexico, in 1821, successfully shed itself of Spanish rule.

The new Mexican government ratified the Spanish agreement with Moses Austin, and American colonists, under Austin's son Stephen, began flowing into sparsely settled East and central Texas. They soon outnumbered Hispanics in the province by ten to one.

One of the few American-Mexicans to venture as far west as San Antonio was James Bowie, who married into the Veramendi family.

San Antonio, still reeling from the Royalist purges of the previous decade and isolated both from the Americanization of Texas and from the ongoing political turmoil in Mexico City, lost its status as provincial capital. Texas was merged with Coahuila, and Saltillo, south of the Rio Grande, became capital of the combined provinces in 1824.

North of the Rio Grande, longtime residents and newcomers alike felt comfortable with the democratic framework of a Mexican constitution approved the same year.

But things took a fateful turn.

General Antonio López de Santa Anna, elected Mexico's president in 1833, siezed dictatorial powers and threw out the Constitution of 1824. In the fall of 1835 he sent soldiers north from Mexico City to crush opposition.

As at Lexington and Concord, colonists incensed at a distant government's abrupt interference in their previously approved ways rose up in protest. Settlers calling themselves Texians swarmed to meet the approaching Mexican army and, on October 2, 1835, defeated the Mexicans southeast of San Antonio, at Gonzales.

One of the few American-Mexicans to venture as far west as San Antonio was James Bowie, who married into the Veramendi family.

Ben Milam rallies the besieging Texas troops to advance on San Antonio in this 19th century painting by Harry McArdle.

One of San Antonio's leading native-born citizens to embrace the Texas cause was José Antonio Navarro, a signer of the Texas Declaration of Independence and later state senator, whose home and law office are preserved as a State Historic Site.

Then Santa Anna's brother-in-law, General Martín Perfecto de Cós, who had been sent up to take charge in San Antonio, battled rebels led by James Bowie near Mission Concepción and retreated into the town.

The Siege of Béxar began.

More than 500 Texians surrounded San Antonio, besieging an army twice as large and armed with cannon. For two months the Texians, lacking artillery, held back while supplies dwindled on both sides. Then on December 4, as the besiegers were preparing to withdraw, one of them, Ben Milam, stepped forward to shout, "Who will go into San Antonio with old Ben Milam?"

Before dawn the next day, 300 Texians crept with Milam through lines of surprised pickets and into the outskirts of San Antonio. On the third day of house-to-house fighting, Milam was killed by a sniper's bullet as he entered the courtyard of the Veramendi house. But the siege was soon over.

The hapless General Cós, his soldiers deserting as they steadily lost ground to the Texians, gave up. He signed articles of surrender on December 10 in La Villita, a cluster of homes not far from the Alamo. After promising that his men would never again fight against the Constitution of 1824 or Texas colonists, Cós and his troops were permitted to go back.

And that, thought many of the victors, settled it. They left a 100-man garrison behind in San Antonio and went home.

But the Mexican president, Antonio López de Santa Anna, swore vengeance. With the concurrence of the Mexican Congress, he took command of the army and prepared for a quick march north.

The attack began after Ben Milam stepped forward to shout, "Who will go into San Antonio with old Ben Milam?"

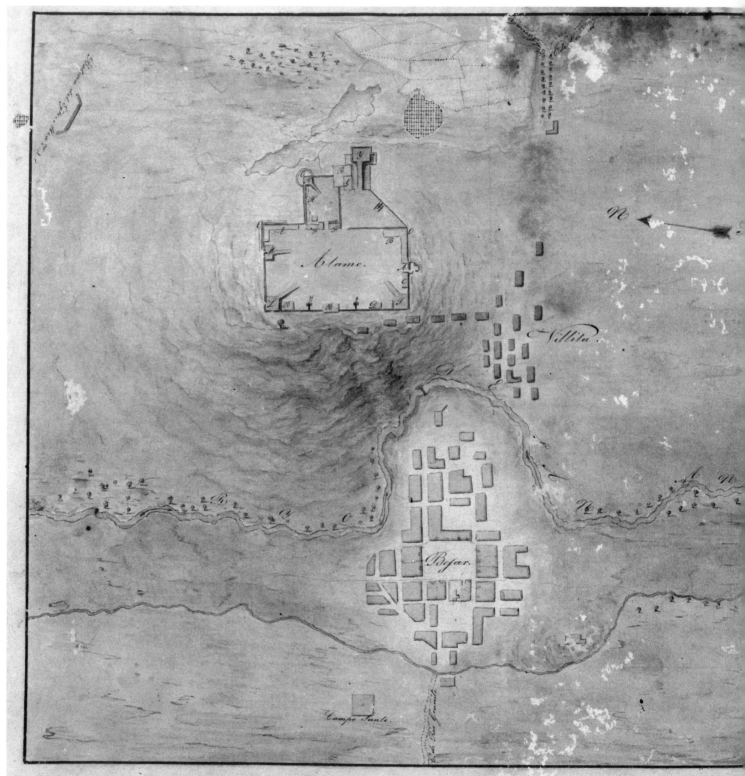

Álamo

Villita

N

Béjar

Campo Santo

Plano de la Ciudad de S.ᵗ Antonio de Béjar y fortificacion del Álamo, levantado y labado
Comandante de Yngenieros del Ejercito del Norte, quien lo dedica al E.S. General D. Vicente Filisola ²⁶

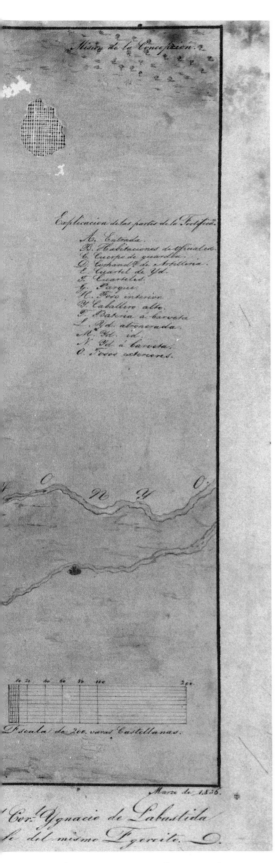

The Mexican army's map of San Antonio for the siege of the Alamo.

3. An Independent Texas

Santa Anna's lightning strike to avenge his brother-in-law's defeat very nearly succeeded at the outset. The garrison in San Antonio barely had time to scurry behind the old mission walls of the Alamo before the Mexican army came into town on February 23, 1836.

The plan was to execute or exile colonists taking part in the uprising and to relocate the rest of them in the Mexican interior.

Most of the Texas militia was elsewhere. Its commander, Sam Houston, was at Washington-on-the-Brazos working with other leaders to form a provisional government.

There followed one of those events that resonates through world history as an example of valor in the defense of liberty against impossible odds.

In a plea for reinforcements "To the People of Texas and All Americans in the World," the garrison's commander, William Barret Travis, swore, "I shall never surrender or retreat." Travis, 25, a former Alabama lawyer and independence firebrand from East Texas, had received sole command of the troops from the ailing James Bowie, 40, a Tennesee-born frontiersman whose brother invented the Bowie knife.

Notables among the other nearly 200 men behind the Alamo walls were ex-Tennessee congressman David Crockett, 49, and Travis's schoolmate and fellow Alabama lawyer James Butler Bonham, 28. Another lawyer, Yale-educated South Carolinian Samuel Augustus Maverick, 32, was sent along with North Carolinian Jesse Badgett, 29, to sign a declaration of independence on behalf of the garrison and to plea for more reinforcements.

Little help, however, was forthcoming. The revolutionary leaders at Washington-on-the-Brazos, expecting the Alamo defenders to retreat, were preoccupied with signing—on March 2—the Texas Declaration of

Fall of the Alamo, *a painting completed by Theodore Gentilz in 1885.*

After a 13-day siege, the third Mexican assault broke through the Alamo walls.

Independence, forming a government and drafting a constitution for the Republic of Texas.

On March 6, after a 13-day siege that took a heavy toll on the Mexican force, the third Mexican assault broke through the Alamo walls. Santa Anna, true to his promise, saw that all defenders were slain. A few non-combatants were released to spread the news. Even though the fight at the Alamo put his army in disarray, Santa Anna headed east to finish his job.

A month and a half later, on April 21, 1836, Sam Houston's fresh troops outmaneuvered Santa Anna at San Jacinto. Santa Anna was not only defeated but captured. He was freed only after he recognized Texas independence.

The earliest known and datable photograph taken in the State of Texas is this daguerrotype of the Alamo church in 1849, the year before the battle-scarred structure was roofed by the U.S. Army and its famous gabled parapet was added. The mirror image of the daguerrotype is here reversed, showing the subject as seen by the photographer.

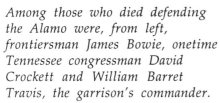

Among those who died defending the Alamo were, from left, frontiersman James Bowie, onetime Tennessee congressman David Crockett and William Barret Travis, the garrison's commander.

The Republic of Texas did not bring San Antonio much relief from strife. The isolated town remained an easy target for Indian raids.

In 1840 a peace effort went awry when Comanche chiefs showed up at the old Spanish Council House on Main Plaza with only two of the 200 captives they had taken. Tempers flared, shots rang out and in the ensuing melee 35 Indians—chiefs, women and children—and seven whites—including a local judge and the sheriff—were killed. The debacle complicated Indian relations for years to come.

Dangers from Indian raids were compounded by fears of invasion from Mexico, which could not bring itself to accept the loss of Texas. In March of 1842 one general sought to display Mexican sovereignty over Texas by marching up with 600 soldiers. He took San Antonio, raised the Mexican flag and left after occupying the town for two days.

Six months later, a Mexican army twice as large and led by Adrian Woll, a French-born soldier of fortune, siezed and looted San Antonio. Woll retreated in the face of a Texas force, but he took with him some 50 San Antonio officials and prominent citizens for a stay in Mexico's Perote Prison.

Not knowing whether they would next face an Indian tomahawk or a Mexican musket, most remaining women and children fled San Antonio. Its population, which had been 3,000 forty years before, dropped to 800.

Nor did the republic's long-sought annexation by the United States bring beleagured San Antonio immediate relief.

4. A "Jumble of Races"

Even when Texas in 1845 became the 26th state in the United States, San Antonio was not secure. There would be one more war before the city could rise from its torpor, for the annexation of Texas brought an immediate and hostile response from the government of Mexico, still unable to accept its loss.

The Mexican War was fought far from San Antonio. But the 800 persons who remained kept to themselves, fearing new invasions and tumult.

In 1849, a year after the war ended, the young future President Rutherford B. Hayes rode through San Antonio on horseback and saw "an old, ruined Spanish town."

But with Mexico no longer a threat and the U.S. Army guaranteeing protection from Indian raids, old and new residents poured back into San Antonio, in one decade raising its population 10 times to more than 8,000. Joining the longtime mix of Hispanic and Anglo-American residents were immigrants from Germany, France, Italy, England, Denmark and a host of other countries.

Their presence kept San Antonio from being transformed into a traditional American frontier boom town of few ethnic groups, intensifying, rather, its "odd and antiquated foreignness" and leaving a legacy that still distinguishes San Antonio from other American cities.

As in Spanish times, broad economic growth for San Antonio was thwarted by geography. Still an arduous overland journey from the rest of civilization, the town's usefulness remained as a strategic military outpost, and as the center of a small ranching industry struggling to develop routes to distant markets.

The U.S. Army moved quickly to establish San Antonio as a military center. Even before annexation of Texas was formally approved the army had moved in and set up headquarters in what was left of the old Spanish barracks

Joining the old steeple of San Fernando, left, on the San Antonio skyline is the bell tower of the new St. Mary's Catholic Church in Hermann Lungkwitz's "Crockett Street Looking West" (1857). Standing in the doorway may be the homeowner, Mayor W.C.A. Thielepape. The man carrying the saw would be his across-the-street neighbor, cabinetmaker Wenzel Friedrich. A fountain is now in the center of the intersection, with the Alamo to the right and the Menger Hotel to the left.

San Antonio enjoyed record growth once it was protected from Mexican invasions and Indian raids by the U.S. Army, which used the Alamo, left below, as a depot to supply frontier forts. Oxen, horses and mules also pulled civilian baggage, as on Main Plaza, its northwest corner shown at left above. German immigrants clustered near the river in La Villita, above, dominated by the spire of St. John's Lutheran Church, built in 1852.

on Military Plaza, later leasing the deserted Alamo buildings from the Catholic Church as a supply depot and beginning an arsenal complex across town.

Now there were profits to be made contracting with the army to sell and transport supplies to forts along the Rio Grande and on the Indian frontier. San Antonio soon could boast a small civilian merchant elite, mostly Irish-born. Merchants could also supply mule trains passing through from Texas coastal ports to gold and silver mines in territories to the west, and along reestablished routes into Mexico.

San Antonio also got what may have been the nation's first cross-country transport service to the west coast. In 1857, Concord stagecoaches drawn by four-horse teams began carrying mail and passengers between San Antonio and San Diego, a 27 day, 1,500-mile trip that cost one-way travelers $200—in modern currency, $3,100.

What travelers found in a San Antonio dominated by no single ethnic group and having to rely on native building materials was, as Olmsted wrote, "a jumble of races, costumes, languages and buildings." Another observer, Richard Everett, who came through in 1858 with a mule-drawn supply train bound from the Texas coast for silver mines in Arizona, thought San Antonio more like Quebec than like any place in the United States.

"Walking about the city and its environs, you may well fancy yourself in some strange land," Everett wrote. "The narrow streets, the stout old walls which seem determined not to crumble away, . . . the dark, banditti-like figures that gaze at you from the low doorways . . . bespeak a condition

Adding zest to pre–Civil War San Antonio were fandangos, like the one recorded at left in the Spanish Governor's Palace by Theodore Gentilz in 1848, and below, cockfights, their noise often drowning out church services. The boisterous Bob Augustine, however, grabbed too much gusto. For "behavior unbecoming a gentleman" he found himself in 1861, above, at the end of a noose on Military Plaza. Animals at left center are not an artist's fantasy but actual camels, first imported from North Africa by the army in 1855 to help carry supplies across the arid Southwest.

widely different from what you are accustomed to behold in any American town."

Around the plazas, shoppers—often in their native dress and speaking native tongues—walked dusty streets lined with low buildings as varied in appearance as the people, while government mule trains lumbered out and stagecoaches clattered in with passengers and mail. An occasional Indian "in his finery" rode in "on a shaggy horse in search of blankets, powder and ball."

At night, soldiers and muleteers mingled with the locals around torchlit stands selling tortillas, tamales and whiskey. "Mountebanks" with drums and trombones sometimes paraded by. At indoor fandangos, fiddlers by the light of candles and lanterns played boleros or polkas, the music punctuated now and then by a reveler's gunshot fired in the air.

Warned one visitor, Frederick Law Olmsted: "Where borderers and idle soldiers are hanging about drinking-places, and where different races mingle on unequal terms, assassinations must be expected." He added, more directly: "Murders, from avarice or revenge, are common here."

Sundays seemed only slightly more subdued. One Sunday before mass at San Fernando a passerby noticed two

Prosperity in the 1850s began to change the face of frontier San Antonio. At left is Casino Hall, its entertainment thought the finest west of New Orleans. At left below is the Commerce Street home and business of gun dealer Charles Hummel, and to its right the home of metalworker John Beckmann. A showplace home, right, with crystal chandeliers and 16-foot ceilings, was built in 1847 by the French-born baker and vintner François Guilbeau Jr. From 1876 to 1878 Guilbeau, also French consul in San Antonio, shipped several hundred tons of Texas mustang grapevine cuttings to France to replace disease-ridden roots, saving the European wine industry.

The Methodist Rev. John Wesley DeVilbiss had difficulty preaching above the noise of cockfights outside.

men "kneeling near the door in a pious attitude, which would doubtless have appeared very sober and Christianlike had not each one held a smart gamecock beneath his arms." Cockfights, he learned, were well attended behind the church after services.

Beneath this boisterous overlay a new order was coalescing, one that would build upon but not obliterate the Spanish heritage of a town that had so frequently trembled to the onslaught of death, war, pestilence and destruction.

For more than a century the crude steeple of the Hispanic church of San Fernando gave travelers their first glimpse of San Antonio. In 1857 the skyline gained the bell tower of St. Mary's Catholic Church, built by Irish Catholics. German Catholics added the graceful Bavarian St. Joseph's Church. Polish Catholics and Italian Catholics later built churches of their own.

Presbyterians set up San Antonio's first Protestant church in an adobe building in 1846, but the Rev. John McCullough did not have an easy time of it. "Every effort was made by ungodly Americans to induce me to leave," he complained later. "The town was overrun by a devilish set of men and gamblers." The Methodist circuit-riding Rev. John Wesley DeVilbiss had difficulty preaching above the noise of cockfights outside.

The civilizing influence of religion was also added to San Antonio's free public schools, a system for its time the finest in Texas. Girls of all faiths could attend the school opened in 1851 by nuns from the Ursuline order in Galveston and New Orleans. French priests opened the

Two Catholic schools established along the San Antonio River in the 1850s were the Ursuline Academy for girls—restored as the Southwest Craft Center—and, downstream, left below, St. Louis Academy for boys, restored as La Mansion del Rio Hotel. On South Alamo Street near the German neighborhood was the private German-English School, above, its buildings restored as a conference center for the Plaza San Antonio Hotel.

German became the dominant language in San Antonio in the 1850s.

---

boys' St. Louis Academy, predecessor of St. Mary's University, the next year. In 1858 came the nondenominational German-English School, sponsored by the city's German community.

German Lutherans managed to build St. John's Church at the edge of La Villita in 1852. Seven years later Episcopalians laid the cornerstone of St. Mark's Church, designed by Richard Upjohn, architect of Trinity Church at the head of New York City's Wall Street.

Germans displaced by ferment in their home country became so numerous in the 1850s that San Antonio's predominant language became not Spanish nor English but German. The clannish Germans became not only intellectual leaders of the city but economic and social leaders as well; their Casino Hall, built in 1857, became the finest center for music and entertainment west of New Orleans.

German immigrant and brewer William Menger opened his two-story cut stone Menger Hotel in 1859 on the newly developing Alamo Plaza, across town from the cluster of lesser hotels dominated by the Plaza House on Main Plaza. Sam Houston thought the Menger the most civilized place in Texas.

Despite all the growth, San Antonio's isolated inland location still made it hard to reach major markets and limited its industrial potential. San Antonio's largest industry in 1860 was William Menger's five-year-old Western Brewery, the first commercial brewery in Texas.

Too, while rushing rivers powered vast industries elsewhere, the winding San Antonio River could not power mills large enough for more than local needs. It could provide the Spanish-built acequia system with sufficient water—that, in turn, spawned periodic epidemics of cholera and typhoid. One such epidemic in 1869 would be treated by the city's first hospital, Santa Rosa Infirmary—predecessor of Santa Rosa Hospital—just opened by the Sisters of Charity of the Incarnate Word, newly arrived from Galveston.

With a relatively large population but still only a service-based economy, San Antonio's per capita wealth stood far below that of the other major but smaller Texas cities—Galveston, Houston and Austin.

San Antonians had some answers on breaking through to the outside world. In 1850 leading citizens managed to get a charter for a railroad from the coastal ports of Port Lavaca and Indianola to San Antonio.

But construction of the San Antonio and Mexican Gulf Railroad had crept scarcely 25 miles inland by 1861, when yet another cataclysm spread new disruption to the city.

Charles Degan was brewmaster for William Menger's brewery, left, housed in a cellar reached by a tunnel from the elegant Menger Hotel, which opened in 1859 on Alamo Plaza.

Formal surrender of federal troops in Texas to a local militia carrying the Bonnie Blue Flag, an early banner of secession, occurred on February 16, 1861, on Main Plaza, as some spectators watched from the balcony of the Plaza House Hotel. Carl von Iwonski, who sketched the scene for "Harper's Weekly," was one of several artists through the years to improve on the apearance of the original bell tower of the San Fernando church.

5. Civil War

On the western fringe of what was coalescing as the Confederate States of America, San Antonio lacked overwhelming support for secession. It passed in the city by only 3 percent. Sam Houston, the revered governor, opposed the issue in a speech from the balcony of the Plaza House.

When it appeared that secession would carry, General David E. Twiggs, who commanded Texas forces from headquarters at San Antonio's new U.S. Arsenal, was persuaded to avoid bloodshed by surrendering his troops and supplies to local southern sympathizers a week before Texas voters approved secession.

Twiggs, a Georgian, was promptly dismissed from the Union Army and then commissioned a major general by the Confederacy.

Robert E. Lee had been based out of San Antonio as a regimental commander at frontier forts for five years. A familiar figure in the city, he left several local sites claiming to be the place where he made his final decision to join the Confederate Army.

The decision was easier for Ohio-born Charles Anderson, whose ranchhouse was the future Argyle Club in Alamo Heights and whose brother commanded Union troops at Fort Sumter. He departed after a visit from a group of southern-sympathizing vigilantes.

The issue was particularly troubling for many German immigrants who opposed slavery and who had come to San Antonio and the surrounding countryside to escape warfare, not to get into the middle of it once again. A number of them disputing Confederate conscription laws were shot or hanged.

Despite all this, San Antonio fared relatively well during the war. Until the Union blockade of the Mississippi River and the Gulf Coast, San Antonians prospered by driving cattle east to feed Confederate armies. Tons of

Secession passed in San Antonio by a majority of 3 percent.

Tillie Brackenridge, brought to San Antonio as a slave by the Vance family, recalled Robert E. Lee as a frequent guest in the Vance home before the Civil War.

gunpowder shipped up from Mexico was made into ammunition and shipped east as well.

Incoming retail goods became harder to find in San Antonio, and Mexican silver coinage was preferred over Confederate currency. But the wartime blockades did not end the city's relative trade prosperity. Confederate cotton simply went through the other way, slipped across the Rio Grande to neutral Mexico and out of the port of Matamoras to Europe.

When Union forces prepared to seal off the Rio Grande, the legendary Texas Ranger John S. (Rip) Ford gathered several hundred draft-exempt men and young boys in San Antonio and led them south. Aware of Lee's surrender but determined to continue the struggle, they defeated a Union force at the Battle of Palmito Ranch on May 13, 1865. It was the last land action of the Civil War.

With the war over, wounds were not as deep in San Antonio as in parts of the Confederacy farther east. San Antonio could pick up the pace of a frontier boomtown where it left off.

William Vance's two-story building on the future site of the Gunter Hotel was local head-quarters for the Confederate Army during the Civil War. Robert E. Lee was a frequent visitor at Vance's Greek Revival limestone block home, shown in a later incarnation as an art school. The house was completed in 1859 on the future site of a Federal Reserve bank. The quality of its construction, with columned galleries front and rear, cause architectural historians to consider it one of the finest homes ever built in Texas.

Commerce Street was a major thoroughfare for wagon trains en route to and from the Military Plaza gathering point in the years before the railroad reached San Antonio.

6. The Old West

As cowboys and wagon trains crowded the narrow streets and filled Military Plaza, San Antonio found itself with all the trappings of the Old West.

When the U.S. Army marched back into San Antonio in 1865, it was less an army of occupation and reconstruction than one returning to defend the region. The Confederacy had been hard put to man frontier forts, and Indians were once again ravaging isolated farms and ranches. Soldiers were good for the economy.

A resurgent San Antonio, more southwestern than southern, appealed to the likes of George Washington Brackenridge, a Republican and Union treasury agent in wartime New Orleans who did not feel comfortable returning to his strongly southern East Texas home.

In 1866 Brackenridge established the San Antonio National Bank, beginning a prosperous business career that saw him become the city's only major philanthropist of the century. The war did, however, remain a "delicate" subject for Brackenridge for the rest of his life.

Paradoxically, the very lack of the railroad which so limited its access to the rest of civilization made San Antonio an important overland transportation center.

After the Civil War, with the frontier again protected by the army and new markets for beef opening in the East and Midwest, San Antonio found itself the southernmost hub of a new cattle empire grown from the ranching subculture of the Spanish.

In the 20 years after the war, trail drivers moved out of Texas—many of them to railheads in Kansas—between five and ten million hardy Texas longhorns, a half-wild cross between old Spanish stock and English cattle which actually gained weight on the trail.

By 1870, its 12,000 residents half again as many as before the war, San Antonio had all the trappings of the Old West. Cowboys and wagon trains crowded the narrow streets and the open-air market on Military Plaza, as San Antonio continued to dominate Texas trade with Mexico.

The San Antonio Stockyards, above, became a central gathering point for hardy, half-wild Texas longhorns like "Champion," far right, which won a blue ribbon at the San Antonio International Fair in 1899.

Along with cattle, trail drivers took north with them a Spanish-based range language to which they added "maverick," a word inspired by the unbranded strays of Texas Declaration of Independence signer and two-time San Antonio mayor Samuel Augustus Maverick.

Saddle makers, bootsmiths, leather merchants and artisans of all types opened new shops. Vaudeville theaters sprang up, saloons multiplied and a red light district thrived at one edge of town. Gunslingers kept everyone on edge.

"Sometimes the smoke has been so thick I could not see through it," remembered the proprietor of Main Plaza's Silver King Saloon as, years later, he pointed out bullet holes in the floor and transom.

Providing a major labor base for trail drivers and teamsters were San Antonio's Mexican-Americans, whose homes clustered conveniently just west of the Military Plaza transportation hub.

The cattle drivers and freighters—long-distance wagon drivers—took with them to Abilene or Dodge City railheads not only cattle headed for the slaughterhouses of Chicago or elsewhere but also a mostly Spanish-based range vocabulary destined to join the American language: words like *chaps, corral, ranch, sombrero, rodeo, dogie,* even one of local origin—*maverick,* inspired by unbranded cattle owned by San Antonio landholder and lawyer Samuel Maverick, who took the cattle as a legal fee. Left on a coastal island at low tide, the cattle strayed across onto the open range to be claimed by whoever found them.

Soon the range would no longer be open. A demonstration by salesman John W. "Bet-a-Million" Gates on muddy Alamo Plaza in 1875 proved that only a strand of barbed wire could confine cattle. Fences made possible controlled breeding of better beef cattle than longhorns, which nearly

Teamsters like those with the wagon train preparing to leave for Mexico, upper right, could always find fast food in frontier San Antonio. There were chili stands operating into the night by lantern on Military Plaza and, nearby, fresh fruit and vegetables, too. Lunch was free at the saloon of John Bosshardt, shown standing at the right, above, at the corner of Commerce and Navarro streets. All one had to do, reported one observer, "was buy a nickel glass of beer to wash it down with."

Freighters and scouts from the grand days of wagon trains and cattle drives gathered once more, above, at San Pedro Springs Park in 1926. Even then some of the finest boots in the West were still being made in San Antonio by the Lucchese family. The three boots above right, made by Joseph Lucchese, won first prize in the San Antonio International Exposition of 1889.

disappeared. Sheep and goats could now be easily kept together. Land values soared as new ranches were fenced from larger ones.

The beginning of the end for trail drives was signaled on February 19, 1877, when the first train on the long-awaited Galveston, Harrisburg and San Antonio Railway—a link in the Southern Pacific's Sunset Route—arrived from Houston. No longer would horseback or stagecoach or lumbering freightwagon trains be the only way in or out of San Antonio. Travel became smooth and convenient.

"San Antonio can now take a position in the great family of first class cities," declared the *San Antonio Daily Express* on the glorious day. A torchlight parade of 8,000 delighted San Antonians welcomed the trainload of 200 dignitaries, from the governor and lieutenant governor on down. Two days of organized celebrations began.

A steady rush of new and suddenly-affordable consumer goods and building materials—bricks, large panes of glass, iron and steel—came in, along with new waves of settlers attracted by the promise of new prosperity.

Gaslights and mule-drawn streetcars appeared. Streets were paved, some with blacktop and others with blocks of mesquite wood. A public high school opened and a gas works, an electric company, then a telephone exchange. Mail began to be delivered door to door.

A Grand Opera House went up on the fast-gentrifying Alamo Plaza.

The city's medieval water system of open ditches was replaced with a modern system of sanitary underground pipes increasingly filled with water from artesian wells,

San Antonio: Outpost of Empires

San Antonio's first steam pumper for fighting fires was a gift to the city in 1868 from hotelier William Menger (standing in right foreground), who also happened to be fire chief. Built in New York, it went by steamship to Indianola on the Texas coast, to be hauled to San Antonio by wagon train. Given the shortage of wood, fire protection was aided by the large number of stone buildings, as seen at left above looking north from the San Fernando church steeple; the Presbyterian church rises at the left. Commerce Street's stone structures included the mercantile building of Zork & Griesenbeck, later Nic Tengg's bookstore.

which lowered the level of the original water source, the San Antonio River, still periodically rising over its banks despite efforts to clear away dams and obstructions.

By 1883, when the Pecos River bridge in West Texas completed the railroad between Texas and California, a north-south railroad had already come through—the International and Great Northern, later known as the Missouri Pacific. A third, the San Antonio and Aransas Pass, connected San Antonio with smaller places in Texas.

San Antonio's new standing as a trade center was demonstrated in 1888, when the city's first International Fair was held—in today's Roosevelt Park—and the president of Mexico, Porfirio Díaz, sent his personal band to perform daily.

As multistory Victorian facades replaced single-level plastered adobe storefronts along the main streets, and as squarish homes of native stone with wooden porticoes

Lack of rail transportation and strong water power kept San Antonio's post–Civil War industries limited to local production. The largest mills were the Guenther mills south of downtown and the Laux Mill, above, on the future site of the Milam Building. Also on the river was the San Antonio Ice Factory, above left, a block from a major customer, the Menger Hotel. J. H. Kampmann's sash and door factory, left, help meet construction demands in the growing city.

Overleaf: A bird's eye view by Augustus Koch in 1873 shows a still-remote San Antonio growing outward along its river.

came down in favor of grand houses indistinguishable from others in Seattle or St. Louis, there was some sense of loss.

Even the president of the new railroad, Bostonian Thomas W. Pierce, ventured to suggest placing the depot in a new city outside the old town so as to leave the old city "undisturbed with all its ancient quaintness."

But most progressive San Antonians did not listen, sensitive to such barbs as that in a Houston newspaper reporting on the new tourists arriving in San Antonio by rail: "Many come on pleasure only for a day to peep at the old town, and then go away to tell how queer it looked."

Indeed, one rail traveler with a broader perspective, journalist Richard Harding Davis, observed: "The citizens of San Antonio do not, as a rule, appreciate the historical values of their city; they are rather tired of them."

Already a twin-towered Gothic cathedral had replaced the ancient church of San Fernando on Main Plaza. Once the new stone walls around it were finished in 1872, the old walls were broken down and carried out the front door. The original apse was spared.

Within a few years an even older Spanish landmark, the Alamo mission church, faced an uncertain fate. Despite presence of the renowned Menger Hotel, Alamo Plaza stayed isolated from the rest of downtown until mid-1878,

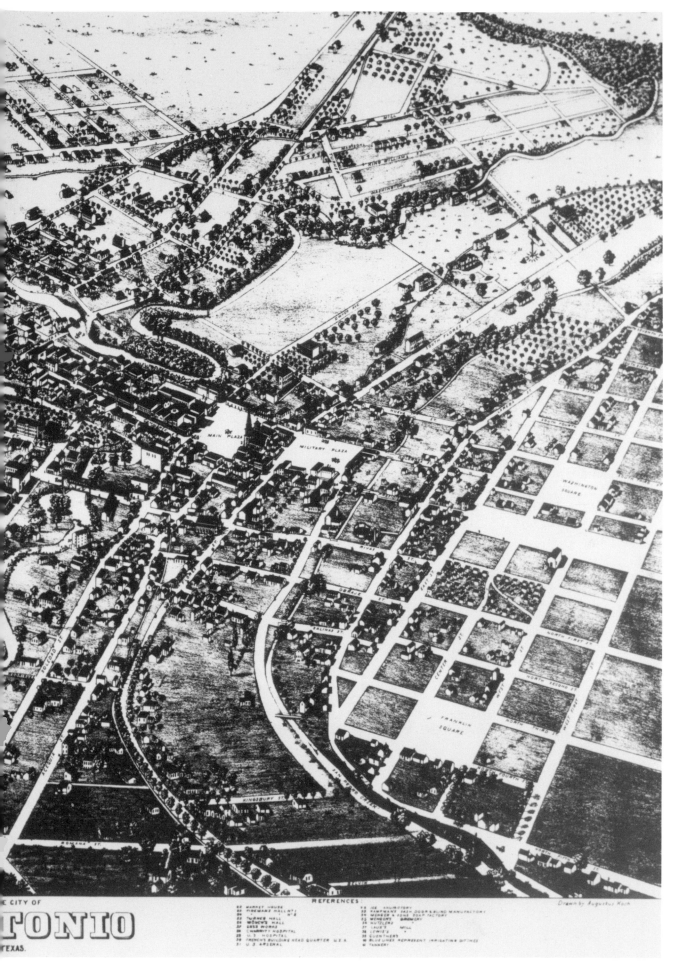

E CITY OF

TONIO

TEXAS.

REFERENCES

Drawn by Augustus Koch

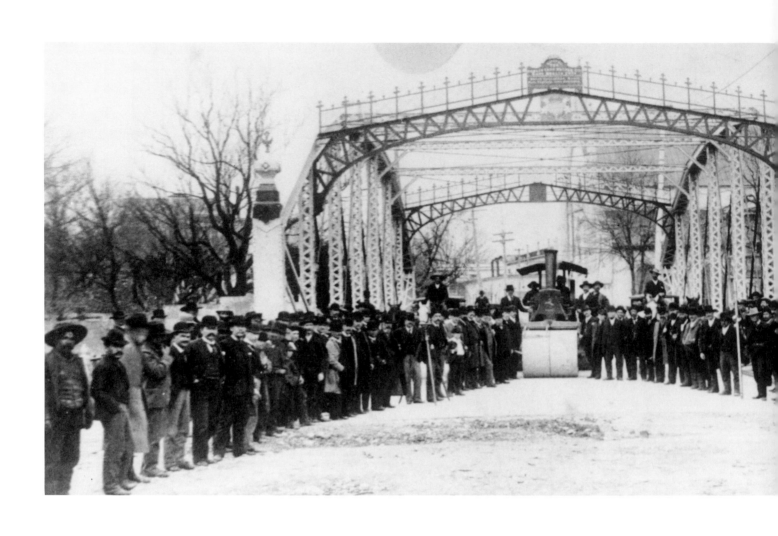

Modern improvements of all sorts became possible in San Antonio once the railroad arrived—including elegant iron bridges over the river, the trusses shipped by rail from East Berlin, Connecticut. Above, the St. Mary's Street bridge—St. Mary's Catholic Church is in the background—opened in 1890 to a test of strength by a steamroller. In 1878 the city gained a rail streetcar line, albeit with cars pulled by mules. The line went from Alamo Plaza, left, as far as San Pedro Springs Park, where one major attraction, above right, was what passed for a Zoological Garden.

when the San Antonio Street Railway put in a rail line for mule-drawn streetcars from Alamo Plaza on one end to San Pedro Springs Park on the other.

With that, a drive to modernize Alamo Plaza went into full cry. Within a decade the old open-air meat market in the plaza's center was gone. The post office moved over from near Main Plaza, a turreted opera house was built and Joske Brothers moved its retail operation from elsewhere.

Multistory commercial buildings included the five-story Maverick Bank Building—tallest in the city—and, by the end of the 1880s, a brooding arched Federal Building with a stone tower in the latest Richardson Romanesque style was being built at the head of the oblong plaza, at a right angle with the Alamo.

While the final spikes were being driven in the rails to San Antonio in 1876, the U.S. Army was vacating its longtime supply depot at the Alamo and moving to the northern edge of town and the new Post San Antonio, which was later renamed Fort Sam Houston.

The army's former landlord, the Catholic Church, sold the remains of the old mission convento and its grounds to a wholesale grocer—who capitalized on its military history by surrounding it with false wooden battlements—but hesitated to sell the old mission church.

A group of local citizens rising to the occasion persuaded the State of Texas to preserve the fading memories of the Texas Revolution by buying the Alamo church itself in 1883. Custodianship of the building was entrusted to the City of San Antonio, which placed a Texas Revolutionary War veteran on duty at the door.

Among the 19th century artists for whom San Antonio's missions had special appeal was French-born Theodore Gentilz, who appears with a beard in the left background of the class he taught at St. Mary's College. His paintings include one of a Mexican wedding party approaching the church of Mission San Juan Capistrano.

54   San Antonio: Outpost of Empires

The open-air meat market in the center of Alamo Plaza, above, was removed soon after shoppers could arrive conveniently via mule-drawn streetcars and a building boom began around the plaza. Wholesale grocer Honoré Grenet capitalized on the Alamo's reputation to build mock battlements around the old convento. The Alamo church itself was used as a warehouse until purchased by the state in 1883.

The saving of the Alamo church marked the successful beginning of the historic preservation movement in America west of the Mississippi River.

Thus the growing hordes of visitors coming by train could still see the Alamo as well as four other popular tourist sites—the four outlying Spanish missions, their decaying remains victimized by the forces of nature and by increasing numbers of souvenir hunters.

San Antonio's Spanish missions had already attracted such early artists as Frenchman Jean Louis Theodore Gentilz and Germans Hermann Lungkwitz and Carl von Iwonski, part of the midcentury European migration to San Antonio. Now they were part of the appeal to a new generation of artists, led by Robert Onderdonk, who arrived in 1879, and others like José Arpa, Rolla Taylor and Onderdonk's son Julian.

All found themselves challenged by what the senior Onderdonk termed San Antonio's "inexhaustible field for the artist. . . . One has only to see it properly to find that everything glows with a wonderful golden tint which is the delight and the despair of all who have ever tried to paint it."

NATCHEZ

An era is passing as the once feared Apache Chief Geronimo stands erect in captivity at Fort Sam Houston, as a son of the Apache chief Cochise—Natchez—sits nearby. In the view at upper left, workers are tearing down the old slit-windowed jail and adjacent courthouse, in its last days known as the "bat cave," at the northwest corner of Military Plaza. No longer clogged with wagon trains, the plaza was being cleared to allow the 1891 City Hall to stand alone in the center. Also doomed, by commercial development, was the residential neighborhood, below left, east of Travis Park. In the foreground are the original buildings of Temple Beth-El and, at right, First Baptist Church.

Writers, too, continued to be drawn to San Antonio's picturesque setting, among them the poet Sidney Lanier and Stephen Crane, author of *The Red Badge of Courage*. Crane wrote of an exotic young woman named Martha, one of the city's "chili queens," who wore peacock feathers and a short red dress and sold spicy food at a table in one of the plazas.

During his stay in the city, William Sydney Porter—O. Henry—set a memorable scene in his short story "A Fog in Santone" at the Commerce Street bridge.

Even as artists and writers and photographers were recording the swirl of cultures that still colored San Antonio, by the end of the 1880s the city's tilt toward the twentieth century was apparent. William F. Cody—Buffalo Bill—appeared at the Casino Club, signaling on its home turf that the Old West was becoming more entertainment myth than reality.

The Indian threat, too, was reduced to a matter of curiosity. In 1885 throngs of San Antonians took the streetcars out to Fort Sam Houston to see the Apache chief Geronimo and his cohorts, who were being held captive at the post en route from their capture in Arizona to exile in Florida.

LEFT ABOVE: PRINTS AND PHOTOGRAPHS COLLECTION, CN 09383, THE CENTER FOR AMERICAN HISTORY, THE UNIVERSITY OF TEXAS AT AUSTIN; LEFT BELOW: COURTESY OF THE WITTE MUSEUM, SAN ANTONIO, TEXAS; ABOVE: FORT SAM HOUSTON MILITARY MUSEUM

Old trail drivers held the first of many reunions in San Antonio to keep fresh the memory of former times.

For three decades there had been more "Germans and Alsatians" than "Americans" in the city, all outnumbering "Mexicans" by more than four to one. In 1890, however, among San Antonio's nearly 40,000 people it was the "Americans" who were ascendant. San Antonio, in fact, had just wrested back from the thriving seaport of Galveston the title of Largest City in the Largest State.

San Antonians set about to bring their city up to the standards they felt that crown deserved.

Appealing to photographers while representing a subculture passed over by the city's prosperity were these children beside a jacal and, above, birdsellers awaiting customers on one of the river's iron bridges.

7. The Largest City in the Largest State

At the end of the nineteenth century San Antonio, no longer a frontier outpost, was becoming part of mainstream America.

Its growth ignited by the rail link with the outside world, in 1890 San Antonio was delighted to edge out Galveston and once again become the Largest City in the Largest State.

In the 40 years until the Great Depression San Antonio's population would increase by more than six times, soaring from 37,000 in 1890 to more than 230,000 by 1930.

As it rushed headlong into the twentieth century, San Antonio would be no longer a frontier outpost but an integral part of mainstream America, brushing aside its past to emulate modern cities elsewhere.

In the rush to modernize, new was built on top of old, at first to little complaint. Was anything historic other than the Alamo church, and hadn't it, after all, been saved? It mattered to few that the upper level of the old mission convento's remains was taken off in a beautification effort.

What was important was that through the efforts of Clara Driscoll, an heiress recruited by obdurate local preservationist Adina De Zavala, the convento property itself was kept from the indignity of being cleared so a planned hotel could have a parklike vista onto prestigious Alamo Plaza.

In 1905 the state took custody of the Alamo church away from the City of San Antonio, and, together with oversight of the new convento property, turned it over to the Daughters of the Republic of Texas, who made the Alamo church a shrine to Texas heroes.

For wider streets in a modernized downtown, building fronts along one side of each major old street were systematically sheared off and the walls cut back, leaving picturesque storefronts on one side staring across at new, homogenous facades on the other.

A crowd filled Alamo Plaza to hear President William McKinley in 1901. San Antonio's importance as one of America's fastest-growing cities had put it on the map for notables of all kinds, including theatrical stars, who likewise filled the Grand Opera House, draped with bunting at center rear. The Reuter Building is at the left.

San Antonio: Outpost of Empires

Wide streets brought prosperity, thought San Antonians at the turn of the century. Already the broad Houston Street, above, with its balconied Maverick Bank Building and turreted Federal Building, was replacing Commerce Street, at left above in the 1880s, as the main business street. Even Hertzberg Jewelry's clock soon moved with the store to Houston Street, where the clock is now a protected landmark. In 1912–14 Commerce Street businessmen struck back with a project, lower left, that nearly doubled their street's width. Buildings along the south side were cut back, and scaffolding went up as new facades covered the scars. Here new sidewalks have been laid and fireplugs installed, but utility poles are yet to be moved back.

The city's most ambitious street widening, from 1912 to 1914, nearly doubled the width of Commerce Street by cutting off the front 10 or 15 feet of buildings along the street's south side—with the rare exception of the new five-story Alamo National Bank building, moved back on rollers while business continued inside.

A symbol of the city's new municipal pride was the turreted three-story City Hall, an exuberant Second Empire–style three-story wonder crowned by an octagonal clock tower. It was finished in 1891 in the center of the empty Military Plaza, which no longer echoed to the clatter of wagons and the calls of teamsters moving out now that the railroad hauled the freight. Remaining chili and produce stands were moved four blocks west to Haymarket Plaza.

The next year construction of an equally ornate county courthouse began on Main Plaza.

The outside world, in turn, acknowledged San Antonio's arrival as a major city. San Antonio became a regular stopping point for celebrities and dignitaries. In

TOP LEFT AND ABOVE: THE INSTITUTE OF TEXAN CULTURES; LEFT: PRINTS AND PHOTOGRAPHS COLLECTION, CN09384, THE CENTER FOR AMERICAN HISTORY, THE UNIVERSITY OF TEXAS AT AUSTIN

Illuminations - Carnival Week

The novelty of electricity and the celebrations of springtime's Fiesta Week—at the turn of the century called Carnival Week—combined in 1908 to produce the Illuminations above, the setting for a night parade with masked revelers. One lighted garland stretched from the tower of San Fernando Cathedral to the roof of the two-story Frost National Bank, in the right foreground. In the background is the illuminated 1891 City Hall with its clock tower, in the distance at far right the lighted tower of the 1899 Market House. The major daytime event remained, since 1891, the Battle of Flowers parade, its entries including, in 1914, Helena Guenther and Henrietta Hummel in an electric car decorated with American Beauty roses.

The San Antonio Schutzen Verein, or Shooting Club, one of the German community's many organizations, about 1890.

Carnival Week in turn evolved into an elaborate Fiesta Week of even more parades, festivals and pageants.

April of 1891 President Benjamin Harrison paid a visit that happened to fall on the anniversary of the San Jacinto victory which 55 years before gave Texas its independence.

Preserving the historic built environment might not have fully caught on yet in San Antonio—nor had it elsewhere—but the city's fiesta spirit of Spanish times still survived, and any anniversary was a good excuse for a party. A group of ladies decided to honor the president and mark the anniversary with a parade past the Alamo, where the carriages would form concentric circles going in opposite directions while the ladies pelted each other with flowers.

It rained on the appointed day. But the Battle of Flowers was held anyway after the president left, to be repeated the next year and the next. Soon participants abandoned the longtime German fall Volkfests for the spring parade week, and the occasion became a carnival complete with royalty, parades, masked nighttime revelers and downtown buildings strung with electric lights. Carnival Week in turn evolved into an elaborate Fiesta Week of even more parades, festivals and pageants.

This time was also the heyday of San Antonio's German community, a cultural flowering nipped by the anti-German hysteria of World War I. Stretching south of downtown, King William Street—named for the German kaiser, Wilhelm I—was home to blocks of homes of wealthy San Antonians of German origin, the mansions

The San Antonio Brewing Company, below left, maker of Pearl Beer, became the largest brewery in Texas before Prohibition, serving such local saloons as William Reuter's well-appointed parlor bar, with its single-blade floor fans, in his building on Alamo Plaza. As does the Pearl Brewery, the Reuter Building survives, but the saloon's space is occupied by a Pizza Hut.

Adolphus Busch of St. Louis revolutionized Texas brewing technology at his Lone Star Brewery, now the San Antonio Museum of Art.

spilling into adjoining streets past the curve in the San Antonio River dubbed Sauerkraut Bend.

For gymnastics and socializing, the German Turnverein—Turners—built a lavish three-story brick athletic clubhouse not far from the Alamo. Four years later the Beethoven Mannerchor singing society built on South Alamo Street an acoustically excellent concert hall— Beethoven Hall—with a columned facade like the newest concert halls in Germany. A lodge building went up nearby for the Sons of Hermann, formed locally in 1861 by emissaries from the national grand lodge in Milwaukee.

A German-language newspaper, *Die Freie Presse für Texas*, was published in San Antonio for 80 years, beginning in 1865.

The presence of Germans meant beer. One brewery had already become San Antonio's largest manufacturer by 1860. In 1883 Adolphus Busch of St. Louis brought new brewing technology to Texas when he built San Antonio's Lone Star Brewery, which closed with Prohibition and has since been restored as the San Antonio Museum of Art.

In 1886 another brewery up the San Antonio River began making Pearl Beer. By World War I the Pearl Brewery—now the last survivor of San Antonio's two dozen breweries—was the largest in Texas.

Elsewhere, Hispanics remained in neighborhoods to the west of Military Plaza, and most blacks to the east of the Southern Pacific railroad. Scattered near downtown's edge were communities of Italians, Chinese and Poles.

Anglo-Americans tended to build around the northern rim of downtown, expanding northward into the gently rolling foothills of the Texas Hill Country as streetcar lines extended into Alamo Heights, Laurel Heights and Monte

San Antonio's building styles in the 1890s were at last reflecting those of mainstream America. In addition to its elaborate new city hall, San Antonio gained a Romanesque red granite and sandstone county courthouse, left, begun on Main Plaza in 1892. Across from Fort Sam Houston is Edwin H. Terrell's "Lambermont" (1894), above, inspired by a manor house he saw during his tenure as U.S. minister to Belgium. At right is the fanciful home Dr. S. T. Lowry built at Broadway and Travis Street.

A half dozen blocks from the new courthouse, in the Hutchins Hotel, left, on South St. Mary's Street, Mexican revolutionary exiles plotted their return. While in San Antonio in 1910, Francisco Madero, far left, declared himself president of Mexico, a post he held, briefly, before being executed.

Vista, where a new class of wealthy cattle barons built mansions along boulevards like King's Highway.

Working–class families followed new streetcar lines southward into the brush country plain to new neighborhoods like Collins Gardens, Harlandale and Hot Wells, near health resorts that drew notables from throughout the country to sulphur springs near the river.

A major shift in San Antonio's ethnic makeup came after the turn of the century, when several hundred thousand refugees crossed into Texas to escape political unrest in Mexico under the dictator Porfirio Díaz. Tens of thousands of them crowded into the old Hispanic neighborhoods of the west side.

Mexican bishops, priests and nuns found refuge in the Ursuline Academy convent. Revolutionary leaders themselves found San Antonio a safe haven and often met in the Hutchins Hotel on South St. Mary's Street.

In 1910 Francisco Madero set up headquarters and declared himself president in San Antonio, avoiding conflict with American neutrality laws by pre-dating his declaration to his last day in Mexico. Madero in fact became president of Mexico the next year, only to be ousted in a coup after three months and executed.

To keep those in exile posted, the Spanish-language *La Prensa*, the voice of "Mexico abroad," began publication in San Antonio in 1913 and continued for 50 years.

John J. Pershing, brought to establish order along the Rio Grande and made the army's regional commander at

Fort Sam Houston, the region's most important military post, was not only a scene of pageantry at the turn of the century but also, in 1910, of flights by pioneer army aviator Lt. Benjamin Foulois, left. At far left, DH-4s from Brooks Field in 1929 drop the men making the first feasibility test for use of para-troops. Earlier, the city was the setting during the Spanish-American War for formation of the Rough Riders by Theodore Roosevelt, shown above right in the center taking a sightseeing break at Mission Concepcíon.

Fort Sam Houston before the onset of World War I, was one of an ongoing line of military leaders based at one time or another in San Antonio.

When Arthur MacArthur commanded the post, his son Douglas became an early graduate of West Texas Military Academy, now Texas Military Institute. During the Spanish-American War Theodore Roosevelt came to San Antonio to recruit his Rough Riders. They camped on the International Fair grounds, later Roosevelt Park.

In 1910 Lt. Benjamin Foulois piloted the army's only aircraft—a Wright biplane, United States Army Aeroplane Number 1—in several flights over Fort Sam Houston's parade grounds. Both pilot and craft survived, Foulois to retire as a brigadier general and the plane to end up as a display at the National Air and Space Museum.

Seven years later, San Antonio's sunny climate found ideal for flight, World War I training for the Army Air Corps began at the new Kelly and Brooks fields south of town. After that, observation balloon training began at Brooks and at Camp John Wise, on the future site of the suburb of Olmos Park.

The transformation of San Antonio from a quaint relic of earlier times into a modern American city reached a crescendo in the 1920s, as it was caught up in a revolution of communications and transportation. Its days of isolation were truly at an end.

Suddenly, access to the city depended no longer on railroad schedules but upon the free will of drivers of the

The Largest City in the Largest State

San Antonio's growing number of tourists after the turn of the century could enjoy the Transit Company's open-air observation car.

new automobiles along a growing network of paved roads. These included the Old Spanish Trail Highway—the future path of Interstate 10—begun in 1919 as construction work was financed by chambers of commerce and private businesses from San Diego, California, through San Antonio to St. Augustine, Florida.

San Antonio's role in military aviation presaged the importance of civilian airplanes, first for mail delivery and then for passenger travel. Radios and long-distance telephone service cemented the ties of San Antonians with the world at large.

By 1923, the Chamber of Commerce was advertising the city's mild winters throughout the nation, and auto tourists were being personally welcomed by local clubs. The Alamo's wintertime daily visitor count rose above 1,000.

The city's long-inadequate convention facility, the second–floor auditorium of the 1899 market house, was succeeded in 1926 by a magnificent municipal auditorium built in the newly popular Spanish Colonial Revival style.

Coming as it did during a booming decade for San Antonio, the Spanish Revival evoked the city's heritage as it defined the mode for new office buildings, hotels, subdivisions, schools, grocery stores and public buildings.

Marjorie Stinson, left above, member of a pioneer San Antonio aviation family, is administered an oath in 1915 by San Antonio Postmaster George Armistead so she can carry a pouch of mail to a flying exhibition in Seguin, 25 miles away. When she reached Seguin, Miss Stinson, at 18 the nation's youngest licensed pilot, dropped the pouch from her Wright biplane so it landed in front of the post office. Three years later, during World War I, San Antonio's Steves Sash and Door Company, left, made wooden Alamo brand airplane propellers.

The Largest City in the Largest State 73

A devastating flood in 1921 left stunned San Antonians on South St. Mary's Street, left, picking their way among the debris of mesquite paving blocks and overturned cars. To prevent a recurrence, Olmos Dam, below left, was completed in 1927 near the headwaters of the San Antonio River, which rise on the University of the Incarnate Word campus below the suburb of Alamo Heights. The scene around the Great Bend, landscaped and channeled by the city in 1914 and shown at right below Crockett Street in 1920, remained little changed until modern River Walk development began in 1938.

Charles (Buddy) Rogers starred in "Wings," filmed at Camp Stanley, premiered at the Texas Theater and the winner, in 1928, of the first Academy Award for Best Picture.

City Hall was enlarged and made over in Spanish Revival in 1927. Even the army picked up on it for San Antonio's new Randolph Field, "the West Point of the Air," which remains the largest Spanish Revival complex in Texas.

With all the new energy, San Antonians made a concerted effort at cultural catch-up with the rest of the nation. Into the new auditorium went the state's first Civic Grand Opera Company. For smaller theater productions, a playhouse was built in San Pedro Springs Park.

A philharmonic orchestra was organized, the city's first real public museum—the Witte—was built, a new building replaced the old Carnegie Library and the Brackenridge Park Zoo got new bear pits and a Monkey Island.

Movie palace design reached a new height of fantasy with a John Eberson masterpiece, the Majestic Theater. Down Houston Street at the Texas, Hollywood in 1927 held the world premier of *Wings*, filmed near San Antonio, primarily at the army's Camp Stanley, 20 miles northwest of town. The next year the film won the first Academy Award for Best Picture.

San Antonians even set out to conquer the climate. The St. Anthony became the nation's first hotel to be air conditioned, and the 21–story Milam Building—then the nation's largest all-concrete structure—the first air conditioned office building. When the 30–story Smith-Young Tower became the city's tallest building in 1928, developers added a 100-foot flagpole to make the flagpole, at least, the tallest point of any building in the entire South.

LEFT ABOVE: COURTESY OF THE WITTE MUSEUM, SAN ANTONIO, TEXAS; LEFT BELOW: THE INSTITUTE OF TEXAN CULTURES; ABOVE RIGHT: METCALF & EDDY, *REPORT TO CITY OF SAN ANTONIO*; ABOVE: *THE SAN ANTONIO LIGHT* COLLECTION, THE INSTITUTE OF TEXAN CULTURES

Municipal Auditorium, above, a Spanish Colonial Revival landmark completed in 1926, gave San Antonio a modern convention facility. For smaller audiences, three years later the city built San Pedro Playhouse, above right, in a Greek Revival style to replicate the facade of the recently lost Market House of 1859. The Aurora Apartments building, lower left, facing Crockett Park, was another in a long list of major landmarks built in the 1920s.

Yet as the city grew there was also an increasing sense of loss, as San Antonians watched aspects which still made the city unique continue to disappear.

In the process of taking over City Hall and making improvements throughout the city, civic reformers in 1914 saved the San Antonio River—by then dwindling to a trickle in dry seasons—with a landscaping, channeling and lighting project along the downtown banks.

Periodic flooding would still require a major retention dam, extensive straightening and an overflow channel for the Great Bend. These would come after a flood in 1921 crested in central downtown at 12 feet and 50 persons drowned.

In 1924, when yet another street widening doomed the 1859 Greek Revival market house, a group of artists dismayed at what was happening to their picturesque hometown organized the San Antonio Conservation Society. The ladies soon engineered the preservation of the San José Mission complex.

By 1931 and the 200th anniversary of the arrival of the Canary Islanders, Military Plaza's once-endangered Spanish Governor's Palace, purchased through a city bond issue, was restored and opened to visitors.

The Great Depression caught San Antonio in the midst of a development boom that seemed as if it would never

The Largest City in the Largest State

San Antonio: Outpost of Empires

As the Depression hit San Antonio with full force, citizens in 1931 line up outside City Central Bank, which failed three days before, to retrieve contents of their safety deposit boxes.

Its can-do spirit smothered almost overnight, San Antonio's business leadership would not regain its drive for nearly 40 years.

end. The stock market crashed on the day the Express Publishing Company dedicated its new building.

Left on the drawing boards were plans for even more elaborate new office buildings, theaters, resort hotels, apartment complexes, a motion picture studio, even, on the city's then far north side, a shrine to the city's patron saint, St. Anthony, intended to rival Lourdes.

San Antonio suffered its worst bank failure in 1931 when the City Central Bank and Trust abruptly closed, taking with it municipal funds amounting to nearly 20 percent of the entire city budget. City operations went into the red, massive layoffs occurred and the city ended its own unemployment relief program.

Almost worse, in the 1930 census Dallas edged out San Antonio as the largest city in Texas, after San Antonio's frantic but unsuccessful efforts to annex outlying areas before the final count.

Its can-do spirit smothered almost overnight, San Antonio's business leadership would not regain its drive for nearly 40 years.

Randolph Field—"The West Point of the Air"—was dedicated outside San Antonio in 1930. The state's largest single planned complex of Spanish Colonial Revival buildings, the headquarters tower, left, masks a water tower.

Indoctrination Division, Air Training Command, Lackland Air Base
San Antonio, Texas, July 19, 1947

8. A City Transformed

At a time of transition for the city and the nation, San Antonio photographer E. O. Goldbeck snapped one of the most popular photos ever taken, and the most elaborate living design shot ever made. In mid-1947, the U.S. Army Air Corps was marking its fortieth anniversary just at the time the National Defense Act was creating an independent U.S. Air Force. To celebrate the anniversary, in a project that took seven weeks of work and used 30 miles of tape, Goldbeck assigned 21,765 men at the Army's Lackland Air Base training center the colors and positions to form the emblem of the Army Air Corps. To resolve optical problems of photography, he placed 90 percent of the men in the upper half of the photo. The first two rows were spaced 16 inches apart, the last two rows nearly 16 feet apart. Yet, at least with a magnifying glass, each face is clear and distinct.

Stunned as its dynamic growth ground to a halt with the Depression at the same time its state leadership role slipped away to Dallas and Houston, San Antonio seemed to draw within itself. The 1936 Texas Centennial Exposition went to Dallas without a credible bid from San Antonio.

It would take a concerted effort by a few businessmen and civic leaders to bring a World's Fair to San Antonio—in 1968—before the city could shake off its lethargy and recapture its earlier spirit.

Still, in the long interim there were bright spots. In the years immediately before World War II the San Antonio Symphony was founded, the Southwest Foundation for Biomedical Research established and San José Mission State Park created. The struggling Trinity University was lured to San Antonio to build its new campus.

Shortly after the war, the San Antonio Medical Foundation was launched through the Chamber of Commerce to seek a medical school for San Antonio, an effort that led to development of the 900-acre South Texas Medical Center.

Also of long-range import, in 1936 hotelier and future mayor Jack White took up the cause of architect Robert H. H. Hugman, who was urging a colorful mixture of park and commercial development along the downtown riverbank. Soon the city replaced its earlier landscaping with a Hugman-designed River Walk complete with arching stone bridges, sylvan riverside rambles and a theater, stage and seating separated by the river.

The River Walk was one of the projects benefiting from the ties to President Franklin D. Roosevelt of Maury Maverick, catapulted to national prominence as a New Deal congressman and then mayor of San Antonio.

In the ever-changing tableau in front of the Alamo, Congressman Maury Maverick points out a sight to Franklin D. Roosevelt during a presidential visit in 1936. As mayor four years later, Maverick parlayed his ties into federal funds to restore La Villita, above left, to develop the River Walk and build its stairways, left below, and to build housing projects for low-income families.

Maverick helped gain federal funding not only for the river project but also to help restore the moldering 200–year–old riverside neighborhood of La Villita and to build pioneering federal housing complexes for nearly 10,000 persons in low-income areas.

The largest of the projects was on the Hispanic west side, where Our Lady of Guadalupe Church's Rev. Carmelo Tranchese had long decried overcrowded conditions. Beginning in 1939, nearly 1,000 substandard homes—many with tin roofs, dirt floors and no plumbing—were replaced by Alazan-Apache Courts, its 1,180 fully equipped single-family units having up to six and a half rooms each.

To the economic malaise of the Depression was added an event unusual for the non industrial city—a major labor strike. A company shelling a third of the nation's pecan crop—grown within a 250-mile radius of San Antonio— replaced its cracking and grading machines with low-paid manual workers, most of them Hispanics working under substandard conditions.

Then their pay was cut.

In the city's largest prewar federal housing project, Alazan-Apache Courts takes shape in 1940, replacing nearly 1,000 substandard homes on the west side. The plight of many of the area's low-income residents who worked as pecan shellers was championed by San Antonian Emma Tenayuca, shown raising her fist on the steps of City Hall during a rally of a local unit of her Communist-related Worker's Alliance of America in 1938.

A truck decked out for a Fiesta parade in the 1940s takes a break from delivering Fritos, a product developed a decade before in San Antonio. With a claim to the invention of chili con carne, San Antonio was a center for Mexican foods, chips and sauces even before the nation's first mill to make masa—the main ingredient for tortillas and tamales—opened on South Leona Street in 1903.

The Rev. Carmelo Tranchese, priest at Our Lady of Guadalupe Church from 1932 to 1953, was a tireless, pioneering advocate for public housing in San Antonio's low-income areas.

In 1938, 12,000 pecan shellers walked off their jobs under the leadership of San Antonian Emma Tenayuca Brooks, a leader in the Workers' Alliance, formed by the Communist Party.

The three-month strike gained international attention as massive arrests were made under orders of the police chief, who claimed the strike was part of a Communist plot to take over the west side. The strike ended when federal minimum wage laws were passed and pecan shellers' pay increased, although subsequently most workers were eventually replaced by machines.

As Robert E. Lee was in San Antonio at the start of the Civil War and John J. Pershing on the eve of World War I, so was a major commander in World War II—Dwight D. Eisenhower, newly promoted to brigadier general—stationed at Fort Sam Houston in 1941.

Called to Washington, Eisenhower left a city hastily mobilizing for the war effort as recruits poured in and as women replaced men in many jobs on military bases.

After World War II, the U.S. Army still bolstered San Antonio's economy. During the Cold War military buildup, San Antonio's five major installations formed the nation's largest military complex outside Washington, D.C. They provided a third of San Antonio's employment.

Fort Sam Houston eventually became the 14-state headquarters of the Fifth U.S. Army, its tenants including Brooke Army Medical Center with its burn treatment facility and the Academy of Health Sciences, the army's center for medical training.

Among the one million troops who passed through Fort Sam Houston during World War II were the recruits marching above, members of the junior and senior classes of Texas A&M University who enlisted as a body in 1943. At right, San Antonio's fire and police commissioner is interviewed for a radio program in October of 1942 as one of the city's old horse-drawn steam fire pumpers makes its last run through the streets before being donated to open the local war effort's scrap metal drive.

A major boost for suburban shoppers came in 1963 when downtown's Frost Bros. began building a branch at the recently opened North Star Mall. It was soon joined in the foreground by a new branch of downtown's Joske's, later Dillard's. Across San Pedro Avenue beyond North Star—in the empty space in this view, looking west—would go a new mall, Central Park, helping make the intersection of San Pedro and the new Loop 410 the busiest in the city.

The aircraft maintenance center at Kelly Air Force Base got the largest hangar in the world and also Air Force Security Service headquarters. Lackland Air Force Base, which included Wilford Hall Hospital, became the only Air Force training center for enlistees.

Randolph Air Force Base, a pilot training center, got Air Training Command headquarters, and Brooks Air Force Base got the School of Aerospace Medicine.

New subdivisions spreading toward the horizon were served by new shopping malls and by new interstate highways and loops. San Antonio's population, slowly accelerating, more than doubled from 320,000 in 1930 to more than 770,000 by 1970.

City limits grew outward, breaking the bands of the 36–square–mile boundaries of Spanish times and unencumbered by the incorporated townships that choked the growth of central cities elsewhere. At the eastern edge in 1949 Joe Freeman Coliseum, new home for San Antonio's Stock Show and Rodeo, was built.

Waterways and a monorail snake around the grounds of the newly opened HemisFair '68, with its convention exhibit hall, arena and theater overlooked by the Hilton Palacio del Rio Hotel, barely finished in time by lifting fully furnished rooms into place, far right above. Three months before opening day the tower's tophouse, right, had been raised only two-thirds of the way up.

ABOVE: *THE SAN ANTONIO EXPRESS-NEWS* COLLECTION, THE INSTITUTE OF TEXAN CULTURES; RIGHT (BOTH): THE ZINTGRAFF COLLECTION, THE INSTITUTE OF TEXAN CULTURES

The next year the state's first museum of modern art was established, in northern San Antonio—the McNay Art Museum, housed in the Spanish Colonial Revival hilltop mansion of its late benefactress, Marion Koogler McNay.

San Antonio's postwar City Hall, however, could not keep up with providing municipal services needed in newly annexed areas. Civic leaders roused themselves in the early 1950s to change to a council-manager government and—under the banner of the Good Government League—dominated City Hall for two decades, considered a national longevity record for urban reform movements.

Municipal services to older, lower income areas improved dramatically in the 1970s, when city council representation changed from at-large to single-member districts, and Communities Organized for Public Service (COPS), based in Mexican-American neighborhoods, lobbied effectively for improvements.

While the military fueled San Antonio's economy, the private sector was languishing. By the 1960s, the only change in the downtown skyline since the Depression had been the National Bank of Commerce's 20-story building.

With little new construction, landmarks were preserved by default, enhancing tourist potential. But without a modern convention facility, San Antonio lagged far behind its potential to attract tourists and conventions.

In 1963, a small group of business leaders picked a deteriorating area just southeast of downtown as the place to jump-start San Antonio's sluggish economy. This would be the site of nothing less than a World's Fair.

The fair would be held five years later, in 1968, the 250th anniversary of the founding of San Antonio. It would emphasize San Antonio's strategic relationship with Latin America by being named HemisFair '68, and its theme would be the Confluence of Cultures in the Americas.

Federal urban renewal funds combined with private underwriting to clear deteriorating neighborhoods—two dozen preserved historic buildings charmed visitors—and build a convention center complex to be used, first, for fair-related activities.

HemisFair opened on April 6, 1968, after some close calls. The Tower of the Americas was finished, though its revolving tophouse restaurant was not ready. A vital 481-room new hotel across from the convention center—the Hilton Palacio del Rio—had seemed hopelessly behind schedule until fair chairman and construction magnate H. B. Zachry brought in cranes and helicopters to lift completely furnished rooms into place in record time.

When the fair closed six months later, attendance was 800,000 short of the projected 6.4 million, and its backers lost more than $6 million. But the city gained its future.

In one stroke San Antonio got both a fair facility and a major-league convention complex, drawing a host of new hotels and enabling conventions and tourism to become the city's second-largest industry.

The 60-story-high tower was a new municipal symbol. The Texas Pavilion became the Institute of Texan Cultures, plumbing the state's multi ethnic heritage as a unit of the University of Texas. The United States Pavilion became the new federal courthouse.

Extended to the convention center for the fair and brimming with pedestrian traffic to new hotels and restaurants, the still-sylvan River Walk fulfilled a century-old prophecy that it could be the "crown jewel of Texas" by becoming the largest tourist attraction in the state.

Across from the old fairgrounds, on a new extension of the River Walk, an urban phenomenon opened in 1988—a downtown shopping center, the three-level, million-square-foot Rivercenter Mall, with 135 stores. Beside it rose the city's new tallest building, the 42-story, 1,000-room Marriott Rivercenter Hotel.

To make room for the mall-hotel project, the old three-story brick Fairmount Hotel was pulled six blocks away to

In one stroke San Antonio got both a fair facility and a major convention complex, helping make tourism and conventions the city's second-largest industry.

In the economic upturn sparked by HemisFair, San Antonio's pre-Depression skyline was transformed by a host of new hotels and office buildings. The fair's United States Pavilion, the round building in left foreground, became a federal courthouse. The larger round building, the enlarged HemisFair Arena, made way in 1996 for an ever-expanding convention center complex as San Antonio's population neared 1 million.

As the city's economic development accelerated, USAA moved out Interstate 10 into the largest single-occupant private office building in the world, shown at left soon after its completion in 1976. Downtown, in 1988 Rivercenter Mall opened, below left, to the blare of trumpets. To help make way for that project, in a move that made the Guinness Book of World Records the 1906 Fairmount Hotel was moved six blocks away, right, to be restored as a luxury hotel.

An upswing in San Antonio's economic growth occurred during the tenure of Mayor Henry Cisneros, later U.S. secretary of housing and urban development, shown at his swearing-in ceremony at City Hall in 1981.

become a luxury hotel. The Guiness Book of World Records termed it the largest building moved on pneumatic wheels.

In 1993, the Alamodome opened east of the fairgrounds with a seating capacity of 72,000. It became home to the National Basketball Association's 20-year-old San Antonio Spurs.

A major advocate of the accelerating economic development and historic preservation was Henry Cisneros, future U.S. secretary of housing and urban development, who in 1981 became San Antonio's first Hispanic mayor in more than a century.

As more commercial buildings were revitalized and historic districts organized in an ongoing renaissance, the Ursuline Academy complex was restored as the Southwest Craft Center, St. Mary's College as La Mansion del Rio Hotel and the Majestic Theater as home of the San Antonio Symphony.

Bold new forms were created as well. Near the former reservoir above Brackenridge Park, Italian architect Emilio Ambasz designed for the San Antonio Botanical Gardens a conservatory with enormous glass cones, designed to bring light into subterranean rooms insulated from the South Texas heat by earthen embankments.

Downtown, a post modern library painted "enchilada red" was designed by Mexico City architect Ricardo Legorreta. The previous library building was remodeled as the North American Development Bank, created by the North American Free Trade Agreement.

LEFT ABOVE: ZINTGRAFF COLLECTION, THE INSTITUTE OF TEXAN CULTURES; LEFT BELOW AND ABOVE: THE SAN ANTONIO EXPRESS-NEWS COLLECTION, THE INSTITUTE OF TEXAN CULTURES; ABOVE RIGHT: C. THOMAS WRIGHT

A City Transformed   93

During 10 days of Fiesta each April, carnivals, coronations and parades past the Alamo draw more than 3.4 million people.

In 1963 Methodist Hospital became the first major tenant of the South Texas Medical Center complex, nine miles northwest of downtown.

Bold new architectural forms in San Antonio include a conservatory with glass cones at the San Antonio Botanical Center, above left, and, below, the post modern Public Library, painted "enchilada red."

As the city's population neared 1 million—making it the nation's ninth-largest city, though its comparative metropolitan area population ranks far lower—the four Spanish missions to the south were linked as San Antonio Missions National Historical Park.

Two theme parks opened on the city's western and northwestern fringes, Sea World of Texas and Fiesta Texas, later acquired by Six Flags. Even farther out, the Hyatt Regency Hill Country Resort made San Antonio a resort hotel destination.

As new developments kept leapfrogging each other on former ranchland out Interstate 10, in 1963 Methodist Hospital became the first major tenant of the South Texas Medical Center complex, nine miles northwest of downtown. The Medical Center gained state medical, dental and nursing schools which coalesced in 1972 as the University of Texas Health Science Center at San Antonio.

Five miles beyond and three years later, the first classes were held on the new campus of the fledgling University of Texas at San Antonio. It joined the city's private universities—St. Mary's, Our Lady of the Lake, Incarnate Word and Trinity—with a student body growing toward 20,000.

San Antonio's largest private employer, home-grown USAA, moved in 1976 between the Medical Center and UTSA into new headquarters, the largest single-occupant private office building in the world. Formed in 1922 as United Services Automobile Association, the financial services company is the nation's fifth-largest insurer of automobiles and fourth-largest insurer of homes.

The 7 million visitors to San Antonio each year included Pope John Paul II in 1987 and, in 1991, Queen Elizabeth II, shown inside the Alamo being told its story by local historian Henry Guerra. Prince Phillip is in conversation with Alamo Curator Charles Long, far right.

New development along San Antonio's River Walk, which has become the biggest tourist attraction in Texas, includes the South Bank complex, left, with a Hard Rock Cafe. A traditional event continues to be the nighttime Fiesta River Parade, with floats passing through the Arneson River Theater, above left.

Another corporate milestone for the city came in 1993, when Southwestern Bell—now called SBC—moved its headquarters to San Antonio.

A different shoe was to drop on San Antonio's future two years later, with the announcement that nationwide military base closures would include Kelly Air Force Base— set up in 1916 and the air force's oldest continuously operating flying base, where Charles Lindbergh got his wings. With 25,000 military and civilian employees, Kelly was also San Antonio's largest employer.

San Antonio's recovery from the shock improved once the city-sponsored Greater Kelly Development Corporation gained title—in mid-1997—to the entire base, essentially a vast industrial complex. It was the largest transaction of its kind in the history of U.S. military base closings.

The opportunity for private industry in the former Kelly military complex, combined with new high-tech industry stimulated by the Texas Research Park, brought optimism that San Antonio would at last break out of the military, ranching and service-oriented economic base that had largely supported the city since Spanish times, even as tourism continued to buoy the economy.

Already drawing 7 million visitors and yielding an annual economic impact of $3 billion, the tourism industry

seemed destined to move from the city's second-largest to the largest. In 10 glorious days in April alone, nearly 200 Fiesta events draw upwards of 3.4 million people and generate $220 million each year.

Convention center expansion into HemisFair Plaza continues as plans are made for even more high-rise hotels—all wanting easy walking distance to the River Walk, landmarks and historic neighborhoods.

For unlike so many major travel destinations, the primary appeal of San Antonio is not amusement parks or resort hotels—San Antonio has those, too—but the pervasive ambience of an authentic past.

San Antonio, clearly, is a place where real heroes lived and died, where immigrants of all stripes labored to build a city that on one hand stands tall and gleaming yet on the other, somehow, around the corner, seems little changed from the 1920s, or from Victorian times, or from the reign of Spanish kings.

A Night In Old San Antonio, a four-night extravaganza sponsored by the San Antonio Conservation Society, crowds 100,000 persons into the ancient confines of La Villita each Fiesta. The ethnic foods and entertainment harking back through the city's past yield more proceeds for historic preservation than any other single event in America, helping assure the ongoing preservation of San Antonio's heritage.

Index